GHj

W9-AXZ-063

The Thirteen Colonies

New York

The Thirteen Colonies

New York

Adam Woog

Lucent Books, Inc.
P.O. Box 289011, San Diego, California

Library of Congress Cataloging-in-Publication Data

Woog, Adam, 1953–
    New York / by Adam Woog.
        p. cm. — (The thirteen colonies)
    Includes bibliographical references and index.
    Summary: Discusses the colonization of New York and its development
    before and after the American Revolution.
        ISBN 1-56006-992-9
        1. New York (State)—History—Colonial period, ca. 1600–1775—Juvenile
    literature. 2. New York (State)—History—1775–1865—Juvenile literature.
    [1. New York (State)—History—Colonial period, ca. 1600–1775. 2. New York
    (State)—History—1775–1865.] I. Title. II. Thirteen colonies (Lucent Books)
        F122 .W67 2002
        974.7—dc21

                                                            2001003614

Contents

Foreword

The story of the thirteen English colonies that became the United States of America is one of startling diversity, conflict, and cultural evolution. Today, it is easy to assume that the colonists were of one mind when fighting for independence from England and afterwards when the national government was created. However, the American colonies had to overcome a vast reservoir of distrust rooted in the broad geographical, economic, and social differences that separated them. Even the size of the colonies contributed to the conflict; the smaller states feared domination by the larger ones.

These sectional differences stemmed from the colonies' earliest days. The northern colonies were more populous and their economies were more diverse, being based on both agriculture and manufacturing. The southern colonies, however, were dependent on agriculture—in most cases, the export of only one or two staple crops. These economic differences led to disagreements over things such as the trade embargo the Continental Congress imposed against England during the war. The southern colonies wanted their staple crops to be exempt from the embargo because their economies would have collapsed if they could not trade with England, which in some cases was the sole importer. A compromise was eventually made and the southern colonies were allowed to keep trading some exports.

In addition to clashing over economic issues, often the colonies did not see eye to eye on basic political philosophy. For example, Connecticut leaders held that education was the route to greater political liberty, believing that knowledgeable citizens would not allow themselves to be stripped of basic freedoms and rights. South Carolinians, on the other hand, thought that the protection of personal property and economic independence was the basic foundation of freedom. In light of such profound differences it is amazing that the colonies were able to unite in the fight for independence and then later under a strong national government.

Why, then, did the colonies unite? When the Revolutionary War began the colonies set aside their differences and banded together because they shared a common goal—gaining political freedom from what they considered a tyrannical monarchy—that could be more easily attained if they cooperated with each other. However, after the war ended, the states abandoned unity and once again pursued sectional interests, functioning as little nations in a weak confederacy. The congress of this confederacy, which was bound by the Articles of Confederation, had virtually no authority over the individual states. Much bickering ensued— the individual states refused to pay their war debts to the national government, the nation was sinking further into an economic depression, and there was nothing the national government could do. Political leaders realized that the nation was in jeopardy of falling apart. They were also aware that European nations such as England, France, and Spain were all watching the new country, ready to conquer it at the first opportunity. Thus the states came together at the Constitutional Convention in order to create a system of government that would be both strong enough to protect them from invasion and yet nonthreatening to state interests and individual liberties.

The Thirteen Colonies series affords the reader a thorough understanding of how the development of the individual colonies helped create the United States. The series examines the early history of each colony's geographical region, the founding and first years of each colony, daily life in the colonies, and each colony's role in the American Revolution. Emphasis is given to the political, economic, and social uniqueness of each colony. Both primary and secondary quotes enliven the text, and sidebars highlight personalities, legends, and personal stories. Each volume ends with a chapter on how the colony dealt with changes after the war and its role in developing the U.S. Constitution and the new nation. Together, the books in this series convey a remarkable story—how thirteen fiercely independent colonies came together in an unprecedented political experiment that not only succeeded, but endures to this day.

Introduction

New York Colony

N ew York was the only one of the original thirteen colonies to develop and flourish under the government of a nation other than England. Traders from Holland founded New York in the early 1600s.

As a result, Dutch habits and influences strongly affected New York's way of life. Although the Dutch controlled the region they called New Netherland for only about fifty years, life there had a distinct Dutch flavor for decades afterward. The Dutch influence exists even today in place names around the state and remnants of New York City's architecture.

New York Colony's residents were not only Dutch men and women, however. The colony in its early days was culturally diverse—more so than its neighbors. To a degree, this diversity continued after the British took control in 1664.

The relative diversity was due, in large part, to the Dutch authorities' generally tolerant attitude toward religious and ethnic differences. The colony welcomed many kinds of people. In particular, the town of New Amsterdam (as New York City was first called) became a lively hodgepodge of people from various cultures and walks of life.

This tolerance, which extended into the period of British rule, could even be interpreted as indifference. In 1687, the Englishman who was then New York's governor, Thomas Dongan, characterized the way New Yorkers felt. After describing the colony's range of religious beliefs, Dongan (himself a Catholic) observed that "of all sorts of opinions there are some, and the most part of none at all."[1] In other words, New Yorkers cared little how other people talked, acted, or prayed.

The Europeans and the Indians

New Amsterdam was, at the beginning, little more than a crude collection of shacks. It existed solely as a trading post for commerce

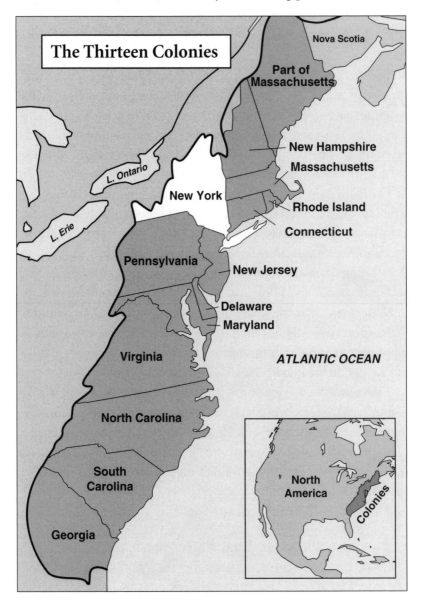

with the local Indians. However, New Amsterdam quickly developed into the colony's major town, and then into one of the primary cities in North America, in part because the town was blessed with a superior natural harbor. Also, it was located at the mouth of the colony's primary river, which the Dutch called the North River but which was eventually named in honor of explorer Henry Hudson.

Meanwhile, settlers slowly moved into other parts of the colony. Many of the colony's landowners were wealthy Dutch aristocrats who controlled huge tracts of land and imported European settlers to work on them.

The island of Manhattan (where New Amsterdam was located) and the rich farmlands of the Hudson River valley and Mohawk River valley were the first areas to be settled permanently. While moving into this land, the Europeans formed a difficult, complex, and often hostile relationship with the various local Indian tribes, who had already been living there for, in some cases, as long as six hundred years.

The Dutch generally acted fairly in their dealings with these native tribes, paying for the land and goods they took. Both sides were capable of great cruelty and violence, however, participating in occasional raids against each other. Also, the Europeans introduced devastating diseases that were until then unknown to the Indians, such as smallpox and influenza.

Nonetheless, in some ways both sides benefited from contact with each other. The Indians traded for highly prized European goods—especially firearms. Europeans gained far more, both in the acquisition of land and in the knowledge of how to work it.

This knowledge was invaluable in allowing the early settlers to survive in a strange land. They probably would not have done so without the lore learned from Indians. For instance, the settlers learned how to make bark canoes to travel the colony's many streams and rivers. They used native techniques for creating trails through forests. They also learned efficient ways of trapping animals, and of fertilizing and growing crops new to them such as corn and pumpkin.

Dutch to English to American

Thanks to trade, particularly in beaver furs, the colony made a great deal of money for Holland. This was noticed enviously by another powerful

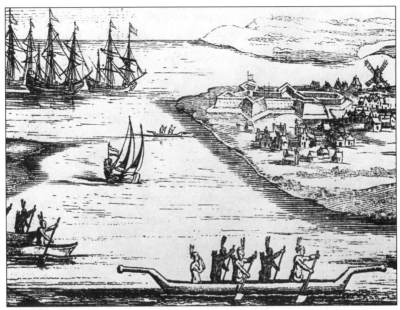

A fort and several small buildings made up early New Amsterdam. The local Indians taught the European colonists of New York how to navigate the rivers and streams of the area by canoe.

European force: England. England also coveted the colony because it lay between the British colonies already established to the north and south of New Netherland. In 1664, using a war in Europe between England and Holland as an excuse, England seized the colony.

Under the English in what was now known as New York, descendants of the original Dutch settlers lived side by side with the newly settled British. However, over the next hundred years the colonists' discontent with British rule became increasingly strong, in New York as well as in the other colonies.

The reasons for discontent were repressive measures such as the imposition of taxes and the denial of self-government. The colonists especially objected to being taxed without receiving, as a balancing measure, the right of representation in lawmaking.

The situation grew so dire that eventually the colonies openly rebelled. When war broke out, the British thought it could be quickly suppressed. Instead, the American War of Independence, or Revolutionary War, lasted from 1775 to 1783, resulting in the thirteen colonies breaking away to become an independent nation: the United States of America.

During this long and bitter conflict, New York provided large amounts of war matériel to the rebels, such as lead for bullets. New York also provided thousands of soldiers from all walks of life for the Continental Army—their ragtag assembly of volunteers. New York's women pitched in as well, performing such vital tasks as managing the family farms and businesses during their husbands' absences.

New York's geographic location also played a strategic role in the war. Its position between the New England and southern colonies, and the importance of its waterways, made the colony (in the words of America's second president, John Adams) "a kind of key to the whole continent."[2]

After the War

Many of the American colonists sided with the Patriots, who wanted independence and considered themselves Americans rather than British citizens living overseas. Many others, however, were so-called Loyalists, who remained sympathetic to Britain. Still more colonists remained neutral. New York colonists were divided roughly equally into these three camps.

Friends, neighbors, and even relatives were thus pitted against each other. The Revolutionary War resembled, in many respects, a civil war. This was true in all the colonies, but especially in New York, which, according to some estimates, had more Loyalists than any other colony.

After the war, these Loyalists were not welcome in what was now New York State. Most saw their land and property confiscated and encountered violent resentment from Patriots. Thousands of New York Loyalists fled to England, Canada, or one of Britain's other remaining colonies.

Despite the exodus of many citizens, after the war New York's population exploded and its fortune prospered. Hundreds of thousands of new settlers arrived to begin farming the state's northern and western reaches. Lawmakers quickly established a state government, and the state's economy boomed. By 1800 New York was one of the more populous and affluent states in America, and New

Perspective

Historian Ray Raphael, in his book A People's History of the American Revolution *notes that the number of casualties in the Revolutionary War may seem small by today's standards, but must be seen in the context of the times:*

More than 25,000 soldiers are said to have died on the American side during the Revolution: about 7,000 perished in battle, 10,000 died from disease, and another 8,500 in prison. This total is not particularly large by modern standards, no more than the population of a small town in Ohio or Nebraska.

But consider this: the per capita loss of lives, if applied to the present population of the United States, would come to a staggering two million. One out of every eight soldiers who served in the armed forces on behalf of the Revolution died; the percentage is far greater if we consider only the Continental army.

York City was on its way to becoming one of the world's great urban centers.

New York's story begins with a handful of pioneers willing to live in a strange new world. The earliest European explorers were searching for the riches of Asia; instead, they led the way to the wealth of the colony's natural resources.

Chapter One

The Origins of New York Colony

Exactly which European explorer first saw the area now called New York is open to speculation. Some historians maintain that Leif Ericsson or Amerigo Vespucci may have been the first to visit the area. Others think it might have been John Cabot, a Portuguese captain who sailed in 1497 under the flag of England.

The first European who made a documented visit to the island now called Manhattan was Italian explorer Giovanni da Verrazano. Verrazano was working for the king of France, looking for a passage to Asia, when his ship *La Dauphine* stopped in Manhattan in 1524.

Verrazano sailed *La Dauphine* around Manhattan and into the mouth of the great river that empties into New York harbor. In his later report to the king, he wrote of it, "We found a pleasant situation among some little steep hills, through which a very large river forced its way to the sea."[3]

However, Verrazano did not explore north along the river. The first to do so was Henry Hudson, an Englishman sailing for Holland. In 1609, a semi-governmental trading company, the Dutch East India Company, commissioned Hudson to find a water route across North America to the Pacific. The explorer thought he might find an ice-free route near the

North Pole, and he thought the river Verrazano had found might take him there. The river is now named in Hudson's honor.

Hudson sailed up the river in his ship, *Half Moon*, claiming the land for his patrons in Holland as he went. He got as far as present-day Albany, but the water became too shallow for his ship to continue.

Hudson met with several groups of Indians on his trip, encounters that were often hostile on both sides. However, he was able to trade a bit, and was dazzled at the abundant fruit, vegetables, furs, and other goods that the Indians offered. Tobacco, corn, oysters, and furs—especially beaver and otter skins—were only a few of the items that, according to the ship's mate, "wee bought for trifles."[4]

Champlain

At about the same time Hudson was journeying up the river, another European explorer was venturing down into what is now upstate New York. Samuel de Champlain, the governor of the French province of Canada, made his journey southward in 1609 from what is now Québec.

Champlain was accompanying a group of Ottawa and Huron Indians, with whom the French were friendly. These Indians were on a mission to attack their bitter enemies, the Iroquois. These enemies were a confederation of five loosely connected tribes: the Mohawk, Oneida, Onondaga, Cayuga, and Seneca tribes. This group, known as the Five Nations, occupied most of New York. (A sixth tribe, the Tuscarora, joined the Iroquois later.)

On the huge lake now called Lake Champlain, the party of Indians Champlain was accompanying ran into a large band of Iroquois. In the ensuing battle, Champlain

Explorer Henry Hudson became the first European to navigate the New York river now named after him.

Samuel de Champlain fires his gun on the Iroquois in a battle near Lake Champlain. After this battle the Iroquois became bitter enemies of the French.

and his men killed or wounded a number of Iroquois with their crude but effective firearms.

The warriors of the Five Nations were stunned. They had never seen such weapons before. "The Iroquois were greatly astonished and frightened," Champlain later recalled, "to see two of their men killed so quickly, in spite of their arrow-proof armor."[5]

This encounter was of great significance for the future of New York's history. Since Champlain had killed their men, the Iroquois became bitter enemies of the French. When Dutch traders entered the region shortly after this battle, following in the wake of Hudson's discovery, the powerful Five Nations sided with them. This ensured the continuing success of the Dutch traders in the region at the expense of their French rivals to the north.

The First Traders and Settlers

Although Hudson had failed to find a water route to Asia, he brought word of New York's vast natural wealth back to his employers in Holland. They promptly organized a party of traders to investigate further. The first of these arrived in the new territory in 1613. They named the country New Netherland, in honor of Holland's alternate name, the Netherlands.

The Dutch were eager to expand an already vast trading empire. They had long excelled at such ventures. For centuries they had cultivated a reputation as masterful traders, and of prizing profit over everything else. Historian Arthur Quinn comments that the Dutch "were prepared to do business with the devil himself if the profits were sufficient."[6]

The traders in New Netherland traveled north along the mighty river, which they named the North River. They were especially interested in finding beaver pelts, then in high demand in Europe for the making of fashionable hats.

The traders found ready trading partners in the Iroquois. The Indians were enthusiastic about trading for European goods, especially the firearms whose power they had recently witnessed. They then used

Dutch colonists in New Netherland established trade with the Indians of the region early on. The Dutch especially sought trade for furs, which obtained a large profit in Europe.

the weapons to conquer surrounding tribes, such as the Mohicans, thus ensuring a near-monopoly on trade with the Dutch.

The Europeans developed a reputation for fair trade with the Indians. The Dutch paid promptly for what they took, be it land or furs. In addition, they were generally not violent toward the Indians. Despite these policies, however, some groups of Iroquois and other tribes were hostile to the new settlers, and the threat of attack was a constant danger.

By 1621 all trade in the region was controlled by a semi-governmental agency, the Dutch West India Company (an offshoot of the Dutch East India Company that had employed Henry Hudson). The company monopolized all commerce within the region and had broad powers to impose laws there. It could claim and settle land, draw up treaties with indigenous people, build forts, form governing bodies, administer justice, and maintain militias.

The First Settlers

The Dutch were initially uninterested in permanent settlement. Within a few years, however, the first permanent settlers began arriving. In 1623 New Netherland was formally declared a province of Holland, and the next year (only three years after the Pilgrims landed in Plymouth, Massachusetts) the first thirty families arrived there.

Most of the settlers were not Dutch, but Walloon. The Walloons were French-speaking religious refugees from France and Flanders (now part of Belgium). Persecuted by the governments of their native countries, the Walloons were eager to escape and settle the new land for the Dutch West India Company.

The group was mostly non-Dutch because few Dutch families were motivated to seek new lives. Holland was enjoying relative prosperity and stability at the time. It had no famines to drive citizens away or religious conflicts strong enough to spark a refugee movement.

Eight families from this original group of settlers were assigned to Manhattan, the island at the mouth of the Hudson River. At the island's southern end, they established a tiny settlement they called New Amsterdam, after the Dutch capital of Amsterdam. A few families went to what is now Connecticut, and a few more to an area on the Delaware River. The rest traveled up the Hudson and built a trading post, Fort Orange, on the site of present-day Albany.

All Business

Historian Ted Morgan points out in his book Wilderness at Dawn: The Settling of the North American Continent *that the period of Dutch settlement lasted only about forty years, not long enough to create a lasting record:*

The Dutch were traders, bottom-line-oriented, indifferent to imperial strategies. They didn't develop strong Indian alliances. Nor were they particularly interested in religious conversion. They built a few haphazard settlements, but basically did only what they had to do to get the fur trade going. They built Fort Orange upriver to receive the goods, and headquarters in Manhattan, that great natural pier, to berth the Dutch merchantmen who carried the goods. When [governor] Peter Minuit arrived, there were already a few houses, and a tower with a bell, obtained when a Dutch fleet sacked Puerto Rico in October 1625.

It was a business operation like Jamestown, a joint-stock company operated out of Amsterdam and financed by investors, who wanted a return on their money. The company sent out governors with detailed instructions that clothed the profit motive in religious rhetoric. They were told, for instance, to deal honestly with the Indians in buying land, and not to obtain it "by craft or fraud, lest we call down the wrath of God upon our unrighteous beings."

Colonists make a treaty with Indians at Fort Amsterdam.

Patroons

Over the next few years the Dutch began to seriously exploit the possibilities for settling the new land. They did this as quickly as possible by giving enormous tracts of choice land, almost for free, to wealthy or aristocratic speculators.

In 1629 the Dutch West India Company inaugurated a policy known as the patroon system. (Patroon is the Dutch word for patron.) North of Manhattan along the Hudson, patroons could take up to sixteen miles along one bank, or eight miles along both banks. Furthermore, they could extend their property lines away from the river as far as they liked. The only cost was the small amount needed to purchase the land from the Indians.

In return, the patroons promised to import at least fifty tenants over the age of fifteen to work on the land. Patroons provided these settlers with livestock, tools, and lodging. Settlers, in turn, paid the patroons back with a percentage of the crops they raised.

The system was quite similar to the old-fashioned European feudal system, when lords controlled the lives of vassals who worked their

The Failure of a Patroon

Most of the Dutch patroon estates failed. Typical was the experience of a wealthy tanner from Amsterdam, Cornelius Melyn. Melyn became the patroon of Staten Island, which is now one of the boroughs (districts) of New York City.

Staten Island is large and has good farmland, and the venture should have prospered. However, after Melyn and his tenants settled in with cattle and farm implements, building houses and plowing land, a band of hostile Indians attacked. The Indians burned Melyn's farmhouses and killed some of his people.

Melyn fled to Holland, then returned with more settlers and made a temporary peace with his Indian neighbors. The settlement grew to about seventy tenants and sixteen farms, and Melyn began to recover his losses. Then, five years later, Indians attacked again and killed sixteen of the settlers, including Melyn's son. Melyn, his wife, and forty-nine others were held captive for a month until a ransom was raised. Disheartened, Melyn gave up his estate and returned to Holland for good.

lands. Patroons ruled their estates absolutely. They controlled virtually all aspects of their tenants' lives, including their rights to move, go into business, and even marry.

The system made some patroons in New Netherland rich, but overall it was not a great success. The failure was in part caused by the harsh restrictions placed on tenants. Many potential settlers stayed away from the Dutch colony, unwilling to give up their freedom to such a degree when they could obtain their own land fairly easily in colonies under British rule.

This problem, coupled with disputes within the Dutch West India Company and continuing difficulties with some Indian tribes, doomed the patroon system. By 1680 only two of the original patroon grants remained in force.

Expanding

New Amsterdam remained the primary outpost in the colony. For the first years it was little more than a fort and a few rough houses on Manhattan's southern tip. Beyond this settlement the island was a vast, virgin forest of oak, maple, chestnut, and pine, occupied mainly by an Indian tribe called the Algonquins.

This changed over time, however, and New Amsterdam gradually became a more permanent village. In 1626 the colony's director-general, Peter Minuit, purchased Manhattan for trading goods worth 60 Dutch guilders, about $24. (Some scholars argue that the Indians who dealt with Minuit believed they were merely granting permission to share the land, rather than selling it.)

As the town grew, outlying wilderness was developed into small, separate communities that are today districts of New York City. Many of the city's place names reflect this Dutch background: Harlem was named for the town of Haarlem, and the Bronx was originally a farm owned by a family called Bronck. Yonkers gets its name from *Jonkeer*, the Dutch word for "young lord," in honor of the nobleman who owned the land.

Both within New Amsterdam and in settlements elsewhere along the Hudson, the colony's population diversified beyond its original Dutch and Walloon settlers. By 1640 small enclaves of French, Danish, Norwegians, Swedish, English, Scots, Irish, Germans, Polish, Bohemians,

Portuguese, and Italians were settled in New Netherland. A French priest who visited Manhattan in 1643 reported that he heard eighteen different languages spoken.

As the patroon system began to break down, these settlers were increasingly allowed to buy their own land. They were also allowed to worship as they pleased and otherwise conduct themselves however they liked. Writer Allan Keller notes that the authorities were generally unconcerned with religious or ethnic differences: "The Dutch took it more or less for granted that there would be religious freedom and got on with the business of establishing trade."[7]

The City Shapes Up

As the colony and its main outpost grew, however, both suffered from growing pains. Among the problems New Amsterdam faced were rampant smuggling, chronic nonpayment of taxes, and the unpunished killing of Indians (including a massacre in which eighty Indians were slaughtered in 1643).

In the town of New Amsterdam, livestock wandered freely in the streets, and the streets themselves were still little more than muddy paths. The city had no hospitals or schools, and its military defenses

Peter Minuit purchases Manhattan Island from the Indians in 1626. Dutch colonists found they could purchase large amounts of land from the Indians for little money.

against enemies were almost nonexistent. Drinking was also a serious problem—the town had far more taverns than churches.

The colony's problems were heightened by a succession of incompetent and sometimes corrupt leaders. In 1644, however, a new director-general arrived. Peter Stuyvesant had already enjoyed a long career as an officer in the Dutch trading syndicates. An imposing figure with a silver-studded wooden leg—the result of injuries suffered during an earlier assignment in the Caribbean—Stuyvesant arrived in New Amsterdam with a specific mandate to clean it up.

A strict taskmaster, Stuyvesant quickly asserted himself as the colony's dominant figure. He imposed harsh laws, as well as sturdy moral and physical improvements. He repaired and extended New Amsterdam's poorly maintained fortifications, including an earthen barrier that gave Wall Street its name. He created the colony's first hospital, school, wharf, and marketplace. He improved fire codes, punished anyone who brawled or used weapons, and passed laws to keep livestock from wandering freely in the streets. He also imposed a 30 percent tax on imports and exports, cracked down on smugglers, and banned the sale of liquor to Indians.

A deeply religious man, Stuyvesant strictly enforced the Sabbath laws, which forbade commerce on Sundays. He even ordered the town's clergymen to give two sermons every Sunday, so residents would have no excuse for missing church.

Results

Stuyvesant was widely disliked for his short temper, autocratic ways, and intolerance of minorities (an attitude that often ran counter to the Dutch West India Company's generally tolerant policies). This attitude was seen by many colonists as uncomfortably close to the sweeping measures of the religious reformations in Europe. A colonist writing back to Holland reported, "Stuyvesant is starting a whole reformation here."[8]

Liked or disliked, however, he got results. The city grew and prospered. Outlying settlements such as Harlem, Jamaica, and Yonkers, once wilderness outposts, were incorporated within the town. A thriving tobacco plantation had been established. Settlement in the rich Hudson

Surrendering

Peter Stuyvesant, the governor of New Amsterdam at the time King George demanded the colony be handed over to England, surrendered reluctantly. He considered defending his territory by force, but a group of leading citizens signed a petition appealing to him to give in. Quoted in Arthur Quinn's A New World: An Epic of Colonial America from the Founding of Jamestown to the Fall of Quebec, *they wrote:*

We, your sorrowful community and subjects, beg to represent, with all humility, that we cannot conscientiously foresee that anything else is to be expected for this fort and city of Manhattan (as your Honor must be convinced) than misery, sorrow, conflagration, the dishonor of women, murder of children in their cradles, and, in a word, the absolute ruin and destruction of about fifteen hundred innocent souls, only two hundred and fifty of whom are capable of bearing arms, unless you will be pleased to adjust matters according to the conjuncture of the time.

Beginning in 1644, Governor Peter Stuyvesant brought order and moral improvement to the colony of New Amsterdam.

River valley continued to grow. Trade as well as the general quality of life increased, and Stuyvesant remained governor for twenty years.

However, prosperity and growth, at least for the Dutch, lasted only until 1664. In that year, events far away in Europe wrenched New Netherland from its founders.

Chapter Two

Forming the Colony

In the mid-1600s England and Holland were engaged in one of their periodic military skirmishes. This European conflict profoundly affected the colony of New York.

Charles II, the king of England, coveted the colony. He resented the strong, nearly monopolistic position of the Dutch in the North American fur trade. He also disliked that New Netherland physically separated the already established British colonies that lay to the north and south of it.

In 1664 Charles decided to seize the Dutch colony, using his ongoing conflict with Holland as justification. He chose to award the land to his brother James, the Duke of York and Albany. The vast tract of land James received included Manhattan, all of Long Island, "together also with . . . Hudson's River and all the land from the west side of the Connectecutte River to the East side of the De la Ware Bay."[9]

The Handover

James sent a representative, Richard Nicolls, to claim the Dutch province in James's name. Nicolls sailed into New York harbor with four vessels and four hundred men and, as his ships' cannons stood ready, demanded that the territory be turned over.

Peter Stuyvesant was in no position to argue. He could not fight back or even withstand a siege, because the fort at New Amsterdam had too few men and only about a day's worth of usable ammunition. He reluctantly agreed to surrender.

The Dutch governor's only consolation was that Nicolls proposed generous terms for the transfer. Among these was a promise that all current settlers could stay or leave as they pleased. Those who stayed would be granted the rights of English citizens, no matter their nationality.

In September 1664, British soldiers entered the city and raised the British flag over the military garrison. Except for a brief period in 1673–74, when England and Holland were at war again and the Dutch briefly retook control, New York would remain in England's hands for more than one hundred years.

The British renamed the colony New York, in honor of James's title, the Duke of York. Its largest settlement became New York City. They renamed many of the other towns as well; for instance, the town the

Governor Peter Stuyvesant leads British soldiers into the colony of New Amsterdam after surrendering to the British force in 1664.

Dutch called Fort Orange, which had become the colony's second-largest settlement, was rechristened Albany in honor of another of James's titles.

Under English Rule

As he had promised Stuyvesant, Nicolls was reasonably tolerant toward those existing settlers in the colony. He did not outlaw the Dutch language or tamper with Dutch customs, even as increasing numbers of English colonists arrived. Nor did he try to alter the colony's religious life, which primarily revolved around Dutch Calvinism.

Under English rule, New York City continued to be a lively mixture of cultures. Elsewhere in the colony, different ethnic, religious, and national groups tended to settle in separate areas, and various regions took on distinctive flavors. By the end of the seventeenth century, historian Michael Kammen notes, New York had distinct regions, each with its own characteristics, including "New York City, truly a social hodgepodge; predominantly English Long Island . . . and the heavily Dutch Hudson Valley, more isolated and slower to change."[10]

Growth was slow overall, in part because Nicolls and his successors maintained a modified version of the patroon system. This system of granting land only to wealthy individuals kept many potential settlers away.

Another reason for the colony's slow growth was Nicolls's autocratic style of government. Under him, New York was the least democratic of the British colonies. He refused to permit self-government in the form of an elected assembly. He did not even allow New England–style town meetings, at which grievances could be aired. Many potential settlers, especially New Englanders who were accustomed to a degree of self-government, stayed away.

Nicolls did try to address these concerns. In 1665 he issued the Duke's Laws, which created limited self-government in the form of a provincial secretary and a four-man council. These laws, the first legal code of New York, remained in force until 1683.

Import-Export

Once the British government took over, the colony's economic policies and structure naturally changed. Direct trade with Holland

Decimating the Indians

As the British moved in and began to populate more and more of the land, the number of Indians in the region shrank. The British were in general not as tolerant of or kindly toward the Indians as the Dutch had been. As the white population rose, the incidence of disease carried by the Europeans also increased. Quoted in Ted Morgan's Wilderness at Dawn: The Settling of the North American Continent, *an English settler on Long Island, Daniel Denton, wrote in 1670 about his experiences in 1644:*

> There is now but few upon the island, and those few no ways hurtful but rather serviceable to the English, and it is to be admired how strangely they have decreased by the hand of God since the first settling of those parts; for since my time, when there were six towns, they are reduced to two small villages, and it hath been generally observed that when the English come to settle, a Divine Hand makes way for them by removing or cutting off the Indians either by wars one with the other, or by some raging mortal disease.

and its allies stopped. It was replaced by trade with England, other British colonies, and friendly nations.

Other aspects of the import-export business changed as well. The fur trade, for instance, became less important. The European fever for fashionable beaver hats eventually slackened, and so, therefore, did the demand for beaver pelts.

Fortunately, New York was rich in other commodities. Forest products such as lumber, tar, pitch, and turpentine were plentiful. The colony also exported such goods as beeswax, pork, barrel staves, flour, candles, hardtack biscuits, flax, hemp, and potash (a form of potassium used in agriculture and industry). All of these goods were much in demand elsewhere.

The importing of goods was equally brisk, especially from other British colonies. New York was in need of such items as sugar, cotton, rum, molasses, and spices from the West Indies, fish from New England, and rice from South Carolina. Some of these goods were consumed by

New Yorkers; the rest were added to cargoes of New York–made goods bound for England.

Problems with the import-export business arose, however. For example, the colony's balance of trade was wildly uneven. New York needed to import far more than it could export. Overall, therefore, the growth in trade was far less than New York merchants had hoped for when England first took over, and prosperity was slow to come.

Pirates!

In addition to legal import and export, a major part of New York's trade came in the semilegal form of piracy. New York City was a major center for pirates, and throughout the late 1600s pirates and privateers were responsible for much of its cash flow.

The distinction in those years between a pirate and a privateer was important. Pirates robbed ships—no matter whom they belonged to—and kept everything. Privateers robbed ships belonging only to England's enemies and kept a portion of the proceeds, with the rest going to the English government. The government encouraged privateers as a way of hindering its enemies.

After the British took over in 1664, the trade policies of the New Amsterdam colony changed along with its name. This picture of busy New York harbor in 1667 depicts the colony's growing trade.

One aspect of this official encouragement was that privateers were often supported by government authorities. In addition, some of New York's most prestigious families invested heavily in funding privateering operations. Such a situation led to rampant corruption. Benjamin Fletcher, the colony's governor from 1692 to 1697, was only one official who routinely accepted bribes and presents from privateers for looking the other way when the seafarers wanted to take a little extra loot for themselves.

New York's shopkeepers and tavern owners loved the seamen, who spent freely when in port. Pirates and privateers were local heroes; the notorious pirate Captain Kidd was a familiar presence on the streets of New York City, where he kept a lavish house. The promise of glamour and riches, moreover, made pirating a popular career.

Captain Kidd was one of New York's most notorious pirates. Pirating became a profitable and popular practice in New York in the late 1600s.

Historian Michael Kammen writes, "The lure of making a quick killing caused many men to desert the army and Royal Navy in order to sign on board a fortune-seeking cruiser."[11]

The Rebels Stir

Overall, however, New York lagged behind other colonies in trade and growth. This, combined with the colony's lack of self-government, made many New Yorkers resentful. Tempers began to flare after even the small amount of self-government they had was taken away.

When the Duke of York assumed the throne as King James after the death of his brother Charles, in 1688, he decided to rearrange New York's boundaries and political structure. He wanted to combine it with the other American colonies, forming a single Dominion of New England. This massive colony would be ruled by a central administration in Boston.

The plan created fierce controversy in New York. Some New Yorkers, loyal to the British crown, felt honor-bound to accept the king's decision. Others, however, were loyal only to their colony—many had been born there, after all. Being part of one giant colony—with Boston the hub of everything and answering directly to England—was unacceptable to them. They began circulating petitions and broadsides condemning the plan and calling for action to stop it.

Bostonians, meanwhile, disliked the scheme as much as New Yorkers did. Their allegiance was to their own homeland of Massachusetts, and they had little interest in being yoked to the other colonies. They organized a rebellion that avoided bloodshed, although they did manage to jail Sir Edmund Andros, a former governor of New York who had been designated governor of the new Dominion.

The Leisler Rebellion

Following Boston's lead, New York organized its own bloodless rebellion. In May 1689, the officers on duty at New York's military garrison, Fort James, stopped taking orders from their superior, Lieutenant Governor Francis Nicholson. They announced that from then on the fort belonged to them and their colleagues.

A well-to-do German-born importer, Jacob Leisler, emerged as a leader in the political struggle that ensued. Delegates from New York's

The Zenger Case

In the early 1700s an event in New York City dramatically affected the future direction of freedom of the press and free speech in America—the Zenger Case.

John Peter Zenger, a German immigrant and printer, began publishing in 1733 the *New York Weekly Journal*, a political paper that stood in opposition to then colonial governor William Cosby. For a year, the *Journal* attacked Cosby, and in November 1734 Zenger was arrested for libel.

At his trial the following year, Zenger was acquitted on the grounds that his charges were based on fact. Zenger's acquittal was the first step in the establishment of a free press in America, and an important precursor to a right Americans now often take for granted—the right to free speech.

British law enforcers burn John Peter Zenger's *Weekly Journal* on Wall Street in November 1734.

counties, meeting shortly after the takeover of Fort James, named Leisler Commander of the Province and gave him full legal, administrative, and military authority. Nicholson, whose skeleton military crew lacked the power to assert authority, was forced to return to England.

Leisler and his colleagues ran New York until the spring of 1691. His main supporters were mid-income New Yorkers—shopkeepers and tavern owners, skilled laborers and craftsmen, farmers, and other small-business owners. The Leisler administration succeeded fairly well at creating the framework of a government, including an elected Assembly, a Governor's Council, and a mayor of New York City.

However, Leisler's rebellion was ultimately unsuccessful. This was primarily because Leisler was almost as repressive as previous governors had been. He showed no hesitation in jailing his critics—who came from both the wealthiest and the poorest social classes of the colony—if they publicly attacked him.

The End of Leisler

Meanwhile, back in England, King James had been dethroned by his daughter Mary and her husband William. William and Mary abandoned James's idea of a centralized Dominion of New England. They assigned a new governor, Henry Sloughter, and lieutenant governor, Richard Ingoldsby, to New York, and sent them there to restore England's power.

Sloughter's arrival in New York was delayed—travel was an arduous adventure in those days—and Ingoldsby arrived first with a contingent of soldiers. Reluctant to surrender to Ingoldsby, who did not have what

William III of Great Britain is crowned king by the lords in the Parliament while his wife Mary II looks on. William and Mary sent a new governor to the colony of New York upon taking over the throne.

they considered proper credentials, Leisler and his men fought the British. Several men from both sides were killed. By the time Sloughter arrived, New York City was in a state of virtual civil war. Leisler, weary of the conflict, finally surrendered. He had been in office for twenty months.

Sloughter promptly arrested Leisler and a group of his men, found them guilty on charges of treason—then hanged and beheaded Leisler and another officer. New Yorkers, even many who had opposed Leisler, were outraged. So many wrote to England in protest that four years later, Parliament, the body of legislators that sets British law, overturned Leisler's verdict and cleared his name.

As tensions between the British authorities and the colonists increased in the following years, the sides taken during Leisler's coup became more clearly defined. Because of this clear separation into pro- and anti-British factions, many historians consider the Leisler Rebellion a precursor to the Revolutionary War—a foreshadowing of the way later events unfolded.

Foreshadow of the Revolution

In the years after Leisler's administration, New York entered a strange period where two governments essentially ran side by side. The colony was under British control again. However, the elected Assembly and the Governor's Council established during Leisler's administration continued to meet. The Assembly even managed to pass a few laws that were heeded. These laws were designed to distribute power more fairly; for example, one was a repeal of New York City's monopoly on the flour-processing trade for the entire colony.

Those who had supported Leisler, primarily the colony's artisans, shopkeepers, and farmers, generally continued to oppose British rule. Those who remained staunchly pro-British, meanwhile, were generally the colony's wealthy merchants and land barons, including the prominent families who had come to dominate New York's political and social life.

Most of the power still resided with the British authorities, not the colonists, and most of the profit from the colony flowed directly to England. It would be years before resentment over this inequality would erupt into war. In the meantime, the colonists had to find ways to survive and prosper in their abundant but brutal new home.

Chapter Three

Daily Life in the Colony

I n many ways, daily life for New York's settlers did not change with the switch from Dutch to British rule. This was probably especially so for those on the frontier, away from the political infighting and ethnic mix of the cities. For them, the problems and rewards of forging a life in a new land remained essentially the same.

Perhaps the most profound overall changes in the colony's daily life came from its steady growth in population. When New Netherland became New York in 1664, about 10,000 settlers called it home. By 1770 the colony's population had mushroomed to about 160,000, making it the sixth-largest of the American colonies. This steady influx of new colonists resulted in expanded development of wilderness and increased diversity.

The new settlers came to already established areas, primarily New York City and the Hudson River valley. However, they also moved into wilderness regions well beyond the settled areas. By the eve of the Revolution, colonists were settled on land as far north as the Canadian end of Lake Champlain and as far west as Lake Oneida, near the present-day city of Syracuse. This extended the colony over roughly half of modern New York State.

Diversity

The expanding population included a variety of ethnic and national populations: descendants of the original Dutch settlers and a steady infusion of Britons; significant numbers of such nationalities as Swedes, Germans, Italians, and Flemish (from Flanders, now part of Belgium); and African slaves.

As might be expected with such diversity, no one religion predominated. The Dutch Reformed Church remained a strong presence, as did the Anglican (English) Church. However, other religions flourished as well, including the Quaker, Baptist, Jewish, Catholic, Presbyterian, and German Reformed faiths. Governor Nicolls was not especially tolerant concerning religion, but his Dutch predecessors as well as his British successors were generally more broad-minded.

In addition to their religions, new settlers brought with them many new customs, languages, and traditions. Even so, however, in many ways the Dutch influence on everyday life in New York remained strong.

A colonist posts a notice giving details about civic improvements. The steady influx of new settlers resulted in expanded development and increased diversity.

Traces of this influence even exist today, for instance in some of New York City's architecture and in such place names as Brooklyn, Catskill, and Rhinebeck. Yankee, a nickname for natives of the northeast United States, is another example; it comes from a Dutch version of "Johnny"—the name Dutch settlers called the British.

In some ways, however, the Dutch influence began to wane. Although Dutch continued to be New York's common language for decades, for instance, by the mid-1700s it was increasingly rare. A Swedish traveler visiting New York in 1748 noted that elderly Dutch settlers still spoke their native tongue, but younger New Yorkers preferred English "and would take it amiss if they were called Dutchmen and not Englishmen." [12]

Work

No matter the nationality or religion of a colonist was, his or her work, especially on the edges of the settled land, was a full-time proposition. Every able member of a household labored hard from dawn to dusk, and often beyond.

Outside the cities, farming was the primary occupation, with wheat and corn the principal crops. Some people found work in fishing and whaling, making good use of the colony's abundant waterways. Historian Bruce Bliven Jr. notes, "Nearly everybody in New York lived . . . close to the water—whether the water was a lake, the Atlantic Ocean, Long Island Sound, the Bay, or the Hudson River." [13]

Trading for furs was common and often profitable work. However, the fur trade became less significant over the years, as the fashion for beaver fur hats waned in Europe and as New York began producing other desirable export products.

Lumber was the most important of these exports, and settlers increasingly found employment in forestry work. New York was rich in forestland, including huge stretches of white pine in the Adirondack and Catskill mountains and of hardwoods further west. The first sawmill in New Netherland was built about 1623; by 1699, lumbering and wood manufacturing were major industries in the colony.

Country Versus City Work

As colonists pushed further into New York in search of forests and farmland, they moved steadily away from large settlements where they could turn to others for help. In the outlying areas of the colony, settlers had to be almost completely self-reliant. They cut down trees for their homes, shod horses, built furniture, grew vegetables, brewed beer, even acted as their own doctors. For more difficult tasks, settlers banded together whenever possible. For instance, several families might quickly build a farmhouse for a new arrival.

Country life required individual effort and ingenuity. If a farmer did not have the proper tools for a job, for instance, he devised a way to make them or simply did without them. Historian Arthur M. Schlesinger comments, "Every man was a Robinson Crusoe. Not thoroughness but improvisation was the key to success."[14]

In towns and cities, the range of occupations was greater, and the need to do everything oneself less crucial. City dwellers could become specialized tradesmen and craftsmen, finding such work as import-export merchant, butcher, innkeeper, dry goods salesman, or baker. Other typical city jobs included shoemaker, lawyer, teacher, barber, wig maker, blacksmith, brewer, carpenter, tailor, silversmith, sail maker, miller, printer, and bookseller.

Helping Out

Typically, men worked outside the home. Women, however, were expected to work hard as well. They were generally responsible for domestic duties: cooking, making and repairing clothes, dipping candles, cleaning house, caring for children, and tending to the family garden.

Often, however, women's labors extended beyond the household. Tending the garden, for instance, might include selling surplus herbs, vegetables, berries, and nuts. Women typically raised and sold small animals, such as chickens and geese. And, although butchering large animals was usually a man's job, women salted and cured the meat— an important task in the days before refrigeration.

Children were expected to help out as much as possible, starting at an early age. Girls helped their mothers with housework, while boys chopped wood, tended oxen and horses, or helped in the family business. Boys often served apprenticeships, a period of servitude to craftsmen, which led to the apprentice becoming a craftsman himself.

"I Am Un Well"

Women's work in the colony was never-ending and thankless. These July 1769 entries from the diary of a Long Island woman, Mary Cooper, then in her fifties, are typical. They are reproduced (complete with spelling variations) in Jon Butler's Becoming America: The Revolution Before 1776:

6 Thirsday. Up late makeing wine. 7 Friday. Hot as yesterday. I am dirty and distressed, almost weared to death. Dear Lord, deliver mee … 11 Tuesday. Clear and very hot. O, I am very unwell, tiered almost to death cooking for so many peopel. 12 Wednsday. Fine clear weather. Much freting a bout dinner. 13 July the 13, 1769, Thirsday. This day is forty years sinc I left my father's house and come here, and here have I seene little els but harde labour and sorrow, crosses [troubles] of every kind. I think in every rspect the state of my affairs is more then forty times worse then when I came here first, except that I am nearer the desierered haven. A fine clear cool day. I am un well.

A present-day woman re-creates the drudgery that was life in colonial New York.

By sixteen, boys were taxpayers and members of the militia; women were often wives and mothers. Even for the very young, life for colonial children meant preparing for adulthood. Historian Arthur M. Schlesinger notes: "Their first and last duty was to walk in the ways of their elders, supplying obedience without question or delay. Daughters had to prepare themselves soon to take on marital cares; sons to shoulder the imminent responsibilities of man's estate."[15]

Slaves were also an important part of the workforce. Slaves had existed in the colony since 1626, and slavery continued to be part of everyday life after the British took over. By the eve of the Revolutionary War, some twenty thousand slaves lived in the colony.

Food and Drink

Long hours and hard labor required hearty meals. Much of a housewife's day was spent cooking. Her daughters helped, and boys hunted for game alongside their fathers. New Yorkers, with more protein and a variety of vegetables and fruits available, ate more nutritiously than they would have in Europe. (This would have a dramatic effect on the overall size of Americans: American soldiers during the Revolutionary War were, on average, more than three inches taller than their counterparts in the British Royal Marines.)

Colonists harvest pumpkins on an October day. Colonists learned how to raise crops of corn, squash, and pumpkins from the Indians.

As did the Indians, settlers relied heavily on local game such as deer, turkeys, ducks, geese, and partridges, as well as on seafood such as oysters, clams, lobsters, and crabs. Most families also raised their own cows, chickens, and pigs.

They also raised their own vegetables. Settlers learned from Indians how to raise crops that were new to them, such as corn, pumpkins, and squash. Other common crops were apples, peaches, peas, carrots, turnips, cherries, plums, and grains such as wheat and oats. Since refrigeration did not yet exist, food was preserved by salting, pickling, smoking, or drying.

Colonists rarely drank water. It was difficult to keep a clean, fresh supply of water on hand. Adults preferred beer, children drank milk, and everyone drank apple cider.

Fun and Games

Life for New Yorkers was not all work. When not working, prayer and church activities took up much of their spare time. Unlike the Puritans and fundamentalists in other colonies, however, New Yorkers generally had no restrictions on such pastimes as sports, games, music, and dance.

Bowling, horse and boat racing, backgammon, cards, chess, and billiards were popular games and sports. Colonists also enjoyed reading newspapers and books or singing and dancing.

In addition to such pastimes and to established religious holidays, New Yorkers observed several now-forgotten celebrations. One was First Skating Day, which marked the point in winter when the ice on ponds and lakes became safe for skating.

Dutch settlers also celebrated a fall festival called *Kermis*, which was similar to a modern-day county fair. *Kermis* drew people from as far away as Connecticut and New Jersey to buy and sell livestock and other goods, and to enjoy entertainment such as music, dancing, puppet shows, jugglers, and clowns.

Since beer was more commonly drunk than water, drinking in taverns was a popular pastime. A minister of the time observed, "'Tis in this country a common thing, even for the meanest [poorest] persons, so soon as the bounty of God has furnished them with a

The Forest Primeval

Historian Arthur M. Schlesinger, in this excerpt from his book The Birth of the Nation, *reflects on the importance of the forest to the early settlers:*

The rich virgin soil, well watered and easy of access, inevitably made agriculture the dominant occupation, and the variations of temperature from north to south encouraged a marked degree of crop specialization. With dense woods everywhere at hand, the farmer had to clear his patch of ground before planting it. But in all other respects the "forest primeval" constituted a priceless asset.

It supplied not only firewood for the household but also lumber for houses, furniture, and wagons, timber for building ships, and pitch and tar for caulking them. The forest likewise provided food: berries, nuts, maple sugar, honey, and wild game. And, to add to the bounty, numerous animals —from beavers, raccoons, and other small creatures to deer and bears— contributed to the family clothing, besides furnishing a commodity for export. The quest for pelts, whether by trapping or by trade with the Indians, became a lucrative business. Had a treeless expanse instead of a massive forest fringed the ocean, the spread of settlers inland would have been greatly retarded.

Colonists work at clearing their land of trees to create a homestead.

plentiful crop, to turn what they can as soon as may be into money, and that money into drink." [16]

In the House

As the colonists moved steadily into new land, their primary need was for shelter. The earliest shelters in the colony were built quickly, using whatever was at hand. Once land had been cleared, however, settlers had the time to build better houses. Settlers often reproduced houses found in Holland, with stone walls and steeply gabled roofs. Doors were split horizontally; the open

New Amsterdam colonists often modeled their houses after those in Holland, using characteristics like the Dutch door pictured here.

top half let in air and light, while the closed bottom half kept out wandering pigs and chickens. This is known as a Dutch door.

Furniture, imported or built on the spot, reflected Dutch tastes in its sturdiness and simplicity. Simple stools and benches, heavy tables, and beds built into cupboards were typical.

Separate kitchens were rare, and central heating was nonexistent. The fireplace served a dual purpose, offering both heat and a place to cook. Kettles hung over the fire, and breads and pies were baked in ovens built into chimneys.

Clothing for country dwellers was as sturdy and practical as their shelter. Members of a farm family might own only two well-worn sets of clothes. Well-to-do families, however, dressed in the latest wigs, fancy dresses, knee britches, and other fashions from overseas. A Scottish traveler, Alexander Hamilton, remarked in 1744 on the presence of newly imported umbrellas for New York City's ladies, "prittily adorned with feathers and painted." [17]

Education

In addition to a concern for basic needs such as shelter and clothing, the Dutch brought with them a strong tradition of educating both genders, focusing on reading, writing, arithmetic, penmanship, and religious studies. Children attended school six hours a day, five days a week, with no summer holidays. Chores were done before and after school.

School was not mandatory under British rule however, and for most children of British settlers education was conducted at home or through churches. When British children did go to school, only the boys attended.

The British aversion to public education continued for many years. The first public grammar school in New York did not open until 1732. Higher education, meanwhile, did not arrive in the colony until 1754, with the founding of King's College (now Columbia University), the sixth college in the American colonies.

Despite the lack of formal education, however, British colonial children had considerable practical learning. Depending on his father's occupation, a boy might gain early on a working knowledge of natural history, mechanics, or navigation. Girls learned cooking, gardening, and home medicine from their mothers.

In addition, reading was emphasized; a knowledge of the Bible was critical, and newspapers were a primary means of communication. British children usually learned reading and writing at home. Texts were taken from the Bible or pious books of proper behavior; typical was *The School of Good Manners*, which passed on such advice as "Among superiors, speak not till thou art spoken to" and "Go not singing, whistling or hallooing along the street."[18]

Health

One area of education that was sorely lacking in the colonies concerned the practice of medicine. The general lack of knowledge about health practices meant that disease and injury were constant threats. Smallpox was perhaps the most devastating disease. Periodic epidemics of yellow fever, malaria, and scarlet fever took countless lives. Accidents with farm tools, animals, and carts were also common.

Impressions of the New World

Dr. Alexander Hamilton, a Scotsman who arrived in the new world in 1739, recorded his impressions for future years. Ted Morgan, in Wilderness at Dawn: The Settling of the North American Continent, *recounts some:*

Hamilton found New York a livelier city than Philadelphia, with more shipping, and flutes and violins in the taverns, and the women more gaily dressed. He stayed at the sign of The Cart and Horse on William Street, where vendors sold water on the sidewalk from great casks. The people he met in the taverns were topers [drunkards] and punsters, bawdy talkers. One of them spoke to the discredit of Old England, preferring New York in every respect. . . .

From New York he went up the Hudson to Poughkeepsie, noting that there were forty different ways to spell it and every year the post office adopted a new one. Albany was still mainly Dutch, with a population of four thousand. . . . All the Dutch thought about was money, Hamilton remarked, but they kept their houses tidy, with scrubbed floors, and Delft plates in the kitchen. They made their own wampum for trade with the Indians, who had lost the art of making it themselves. The women were the homeliest he had ever seen.

Medicine, or "physick," was shockingly crude compared to medical technology today. Awareness of sanitation, antibiotics, or anesthetics was nonexistent. Virtually all illnesses were treated by sweating, purging, or bleeding—sometimes all at once. Surgery was primitive; doctors generally did not perform major surgery, instead limiting themselves to relatively minor procedures such as setting broken bones, amputating limbs, or tending to wounds.

Dentistry was equally limited. Dental hygiene was unknown, resulting in a brisk trade in the manufacture of false teeth. Some settlers carried the tooth of a dead person, believing that it would ward off toothache.

There were few doctors even in towns and cities, so clergymen and barbers often substituted. Colonists also commonly tried to cure themselves with folk remedies from Europe or borrowed from Indians and slaves. These involved ingredients such as herbs and roots, or more exotic substances such as toads, snails, bees, spider webs, cow dung—even the scrapings of human skulls.

Regulations

Over time, medicine in the colony improved and became more closely regulated. In 1744, for instance, a group of laws was passed providing for better sanitation and drainage in New York's cities. In 1760 New York passed the first law in the colonies requiring doctors to be examined and licensed. In 1767 King's College opened the second medical school in the American colonies.

Other regulations governing the quality of life were also passed over time. As a result, by the middle of the eighteenth century, New York residents achieved a level of comfort far greater than what the colony's first settlers had endured. However, many New Yorkers were deeply dissatisfied, and this situation eventually led to outright conflict.

Chapter Four

New York's Role in the Revolution

T he dissatisfaction of many colonists eventually resulted in armed conflict with England, in which New York played a pivotal role. The colony was a leader in protesting unfair British policies. Its politicians helped unite the colonies into a single, effective entity, rather than the weak collection of feuding settlements they had been.

New York also played a major role in the war itself. Because of its location between the New England and southern colonies, it was key to England's strategy for crushing the rebellion. Some of the war's important battles took place in New York—nearly one-third of all the battles, more than in any other single colony.

The Stamp Act

The primary reason for conflict between England and its American colonies involved taxes. The colonists felt they were taxed unfairly because they had no political representation. Although they were British citizens, they could not vote and thus had no say in creating laws that affected them.

Especially offensive was the Stamp Act, which was proposed in 1765. Under this act, many kinds of merchandise, from cards and dice to legal documents and newspapers, would have required the purchase of special stamps before they could be bought in America. Even buying a drink in a tavern would have required a stamp.

For many New Yorkers, this was the final insult in a series of oppressive tax laws. The stamps themselves were not expensive; it was the principle they objected to. Using clothing as an analogy for all goods, a newspaper writer editorialized that it would be better to wear only handmade (and thus untaxed) clothes than to be unfairly taxed for imported garments, declaring "It is better to wear a homespun coat than to lose our liberty." [19]

Several grassroots-level protests were organized to oppose the Stamp Act and other British taxes. Among them were the first New York appearances by a radical group of anti-British colonists: the Sons of Liberty. This group, mainly comprising shopkeepers, laborers, and artisans, advocated physical violence as the only way to convince England to repeal unfair taxes.

Stopping the Tax

When the hated stamps arrived in New York City, they were hidden in Fort George, the city's military garrison. Soon after, an angry mob swarmed the streets to protest the stamps' arrival. The mob vandalized the homes of acting governor Cadwallader Colden and other British authorities. It also announced to the governor that "you'll die a Martyr to your own Villainy [and] every Man, that assists you, Shall be, surely, put to Death." [20]

The large mob could have taken Fort George. Its manpower was superior to the skeletal British troops in the garrison. However, the colonists chose to avoid direct confrontation.

So did the British. When Governor Colden handed the stamps over to the mob, it dispersed. The shopkeepers chosen to dispense the stamps saw fit to resign their commissions or leave the city entirely. The Stamp Act was thus never put into effect.

In the wake of this victory, rebel leaders from various colonies organized their first formal meeting in New York City. This so-called Stamp Act Congress, which included delegates from eight of the colonies, met in October 1765. The Declaration of Rights and Grievances it issued was a forerunner of the Declaration of Independence. The document asserted that England had no right to tax the colonies. It also declared that English courts had no jurisdiction there, and it encouraged a boycott of British goods.

Eight colonies agreeing on a joint statement such as this was an important turn of events. England had always tried hard to keep the colonies separate. Provinces that bickered with each other and vied for attention from their parent country were weak if kept apart. With the Stamp Act Congress, however, the colonies demonstrated that they could band together and pose a threat.

More Conflict

Relations steadily worsened between the British and the aggrieved colonists, who had begun calling themselves Patriots. However, both sides remained nonviolent until early 1770, when outright fights began to break out. One of the first such clashes in New York was the Battle of Golden Hill in Manhattan.

The Sons of Liberty had erected a symbolic "liberty pole," a pine tree, at Golden Hill. British soldiers (called Redcoats after the color of their uniform coats) repeatedly destroyed it, and the Patriots repeatedly replaced it. After several rounds of this, a mob of Patriots clashed with British soldiers in January 1770. Several Patriots were stabbed with bayonets, and some British soldiers were beaten.

Colonists protest the Stamp Act, which was passed by the British Parliament in 1765. The colonists' reaction to the Stamp Act was the beginning of their rebellion against the oppressive British government.

Meanwhile, far more dramatic demonstrations were taking place in Boston, Massachusetts. The most famous of these was the Boston Tea Party in December 1773. This event, in which a group of Bostonians disguised as Indians dumped 340 chests of tea into the harbor, protested a tax on tea that was one of a hated series of taxes called the Townshend Acts.

Paul Revere, a messenger for the Boston Patriots, rode to New York City to report the news. New Yorkers responded by holding their own version of the event in April 1774. Some two thousand Patriots gathered at the waterfront, near a wharf called the Battery, when a group of cargo ships was due to arrive from England. The city's harbor pilots had been warned by Patriots to avoid assisting the ships; any aid given to the ships would result in retribution. The British vessels prudently remained offshore. One captain, whose cargo included eighteen cases of tea, tried to sneak ashore. The Sons of Liberty stormed the ship, seized the tea, and dumped it into the East River.

War Breaks Out

Later that year, Patriots from New York and other colonies organized their own elected assemblies, separate from the official British-run

Colonists cheer as Patriots dressed as Indians dump tea from British ships into Boston Harbor in December of 1773. New Yorkers participated in a similar event in their own harbor in April 1774.

The Battle of Lexington on April 19, 1775, was one of two skirmishes that marked the beginning of the American War of Independence.

colonial government. Each colony sent representatives to a central congress, called the First Continental Congress. It met in Philadelphia, Pennsylvania, in September.

A meeting of the Second Continental Congress was set for May 1775. Before it could take place, however, the alienation between the Patriots and Britain reached a crisis point and open hostilities broke out.

The breaking point came with two skirmishes in Massachusetts at Lexington and Concord, on April 19, 1775. Historians regard these as the beginning of the American War of Independence. Soon after these initial battles, the rebel side scored a victory in northeastern New York when a group of Patriots, led by Ethan Allen and Benedict Arnold, captured the British outpost Fort Ticonderoga. This won the Patriots a strategic site guarding the Hudson River valley, as well as a much-needed supply of guns and ammunition.

Recognizing that war was imminent, the Continental Congress met in an emergency session. In June 1775, it appointed George Washington as commander in chief of the American armed forces. The war was on.

General George Washington takes command of the American armed forces after being appointed commander in chief by the Continental Congress in June 1775.

Barricading Manhattan

British military authorities were confident that they could soon crush the American rebellion. Their plan hinged on controlling New York; the first step was to capture New York City. This meant that British forces would have major footholds at the mouth of the Hudson, in the southern part of New York, and in the British colony in Canada, to the north. By moving north up the Hudson and south along Lake Champlain and the Hudson River valley, the British hoped to gain control of the colony's vital rivers and lakes, and thus control the entire area.

Controlling New York would mean that the rebel colonies would then be split in two, with New England above and the southern colonies below. If this happened, the powerful British Navy could prevent the rebels from supporting each other by sea. Everything depended on controlling New York, therefore. Historian Bruce Bliven Jr. writes, "From the British point of view New York was the key to the war strategy, the main target of the powerful military effort King George directed against his North American colonies." [21]

General Washington guessed that England's first move would be to seize New York City. In the spring of 1776, he sent General Charles Lee to the city with about nineteen thousand soldiers, mostly untrained and poorly armed volunteers. Lee ordered them to build forts, barricades, and trenches in preparation for an assault. Cannons were set up along Manhattan's riverbanks and at Brooklyn, a tiny settlement on Long Island.

The Declaration of Independence

Washington arrived in New York City in June. To inspire his men there, the general had a newly signed document—a paper that would have far-reaching consequences—read aloud to them.

On July 2, 1776, the Continental Congress approved a landmark piece of writing, the Declaration of Independence. With its signing, America formally severed all ties with England. Two days later, Congress formally adopted the measure.

Famous Words

On September 21, 1776, the day that fire destroyed much of New York City, a young Connecticut man named Nathan Hale was arrested near there by the British. Hale had disguised himself as a Dutch schoolmaster, but was really an army officer engaged in spying on the British. He was captured while returning to his regiment, having penetrated the British lines on Long Island.

Hale was hanged without trial the next day. To many Americans, Hale has come to represent the ultimate Patriot for the words that, according to legend, were the last he spoke: "I only regret that I have but one life to lose for my country."

At first, New York had abstained from signing the Declaration of Independence. New York lawmakers delayed their vote because the Provincial Congress wanted to ensure that every county understood the measure. It held two elections before finally approving the document on July 9. New York took so long in approving it that a major figure at the Congress, John Adams, publicly wondered, "What is the reason that New York must continue to embarrass the Continent?" [22]

The same day that New York formally accepted the Declaration of Independence, Washington had it read aloud. That night, a mob of patriotic New Yorkers pulled down a huge lead statue of the British monarch, George III, from a Manhattan field called Bowling Green. The statue added greatly to the collection of lead that New Yorkers had been collecting for some time, and when melted down yielded more than forty thousand bullets for use against the Redcoats.

The Battle of Long Island

Washington's hunch about England wanting New York City was right. In the biggest single military expedition England had launched to date, nearly five hundred ships carrying some thirty-two thousand men arrived in New York harbor that summer.

The British troops immediately occupied Staten Island and surrounded Manhattan with sailing ships. The water was so crowded that one observer, looking out over the vast number of sail masts, remarked that it was like seeing a fleet of trimmed pine trees.

However, the British forces—augmented by Hessians, German mercenary soldiers hired to fight for the British—did not attack immediately. They did not move on the city until late August. When the attack finally came, Long Island was the scene. The Battle of Long Island was a smashing victory for the British. They killed, wounded, or took prisoner fifteen hundred Americans, while losing about four hundred men themselves.

Some Patriots were able to escape to Manhattan. Over the next few weeks, Washington tried to maintain control over the remaining troops, but he lost many of them. Some, frightened and depressed, simply deserted. Others became ill from wounds, exposure, or malnutrition.

Colonial troops retreat from the Battle of Long Island on August 29, 1776. The battle proved a tremendous victory for Britain.

The British pressed on and captured Manhattan on September 15. They held the city for the rest of the war, until the conflict ended in 1783.

The Americans had considered deliberately burning New York City to prevent the British from occupying it. Ironically, a huge fire broke out only days after the British took possession. It destroyed nearly five hundred buildings, almost one-quarter of the city. The cause of the fire was never determined, but Washington commented later that either a divine hand or a human hand did what his army was not able to do.

Three Victories

As the war's pace picked up, much of the heaviest fighting took place not in New York but in other colonies. Three important battles, however, were fought on New York soil: Oriskany, Bennington, and Saratoga.

In the summer of 1777, Patriots were able to hold on to a crucial stronghold, Fort Stanwix, near the town of Oriskany, in the Mohawk River valley. They were victorious despite a lengthy siege and an

On the Prison Ships

During the British occupation of New York City, an estimated ten thousand Americans died in British garrisons onshore and in prison ships anchored offshore—roughly as many as died in combat in the war. Jammed together under terrible conditions, the Americans succumbed to hunger, thirst, and disease. A typical meal was moldy bread filled with worms and meat cooked in water fouled by human excrement.

A young soldier, Ebenezer Fox, recalls in this passage (reprinted in Ray Raphael's A People's History of the American Revolution *his first impressions of the conditions:*

The prison ship *Jersey* moves through the Atlantic Ocean.

Here was a motley crew, covered with rags and filth; visages [faces] pallid with disease, emaciated with hunger and anxiety, and retaining hardly a trace of their original appearance. Here were men, who had once enjoyed life while riding over the mountain wave or roaming through pleasant fields, full of health and vigor, now shriveled by a scanty and unwholesome diet, ghastly with inhaling an impure atmosphere, exposed to contagion and disease, and surrounded with the horrors of sickness and death.

especially fierce battle with British, Hessian, and Iroquois fighters. (Some Indians sided with the Patriots, but many tribes that took sides during the war fought with the British.)

Later that summer, the Patriots won the Battle of Bennington, which took place at the site of the present village of Walloomsac, New York, just across the border from Bennington, Vermont. The Patriots succeeded in holding on to much-needed supplies the British had hoped to capture, and also inflicted serious casualties on the Redcoats.

Both Oriskany and Bennington were grave setbacks for the British hopes of securing the Hudson River Valley, but an even more decisive victory came in the fall of that year. Near the town of Saratoga, a force of some eighty-five hundred Redcoats clashed on two occasions with Patriots numbering twenty thousand at their peak. The British forces were surrounded and forced to surrender. They were released on condition that they return to England for the duration of the war.

War's End

The Battle of Saratoga is generally considered the war's turning point. It prevented the British from controlling the Hudson River valley, and a substantial portion of the British forces was prevented from fighting for the rest of the war. Most of all, the victory persuaded France, Britain's old enemy, that the Americans had a chance to win.

In the spring of 1778, after nearly two years of providing aid in secret to the rebels, France openly entered the conflict. The resulting flow of French aid was crucial to the Patriots' cause. Historian Bruce Blivin Jr. comments, "Without the French money, soldiers, sailors, guns, and ships that sustained the American war effort . . . independence could hardly have been achieved." [23]

The war continued to rage until 1781, when the British general Lord Cornwallis surrendered after a humiliating siege at Yorktown in Virginia. For the British, this was the end of the battle. The Treaty of Paris, a peace treaty signed in 1783, formally recognized the independence of the United States of America.

When General Washington finally was able to take leave of his officers and resign as commanding general of the Continental Army, he did so in New York City, at Sam Fraunces's Tavern. Washington offered a moving farewell toast to the men who had fought with him: "With a heart full of love and gratitude, I now take leave of you. I most

Women in the Revolutionary War

As the war's pace picked up, New York provided thousands of volunteer soldiers from all walks of life for the ragtag Continental Army. Though they were banned from actual fighting, New York's women also did their parts.

Women managed the family farms and businesses during their husbands' absences, and many also formed volunteer groups to raise money and provide supplies to the soldiers. Some women joined their male relatives in the army camps to nurse and cook. A few even served as spies or disguised themselves as men to participate in battles.

In his book *Becoming America: The Revolution Before 1776*, Jon Butler quotes an anonymous writer of the time as saying women were kept busy "making Cartridges, running Bullets, making Wallets, baking Biscuits, crying and bemoaning & at the same time animating their Husbands & Sons to fight for their liberties, tho not knowing whether they should ever see them again."

devoutly wish that your latter days may be as prosperous and happy as your former ones have been glorious and honorable."[24]

Over the next few years, as the newly formed United States began to take shape and to operate on its own, so did New York. The colony of New York officially became the state of New York; it set up a permanent form of state government for itself and it moved ahead into a new century.

Chapter Five

New York After the Revolution

O nce the upheaval of the war was over, New York recovered fairly quickly. State lawmakers moved to not only put a new political structure in place, but also to ensure for the state a position as a national leader.

Increasing numbers of immigrants were welcomed, and vast new regions opened for settlement, especially in western and northern New York. The state's economy flourished as well in the years after the war.

Creating a State Constitution

After declaring their independence from England, the colonies had begun to draw up new state constitutions for themselves. Some, such as Rhode Island and Connecticut, used their old colonial charters as models for their constitutions, simply eliminating references to England and making other minor changes. Others, including New York, decided to create entirely new constitutions.

The committee that wrote the New York Constitution created a first draft in only two weeks, and needed only another two months for main revisions. The process of approving and signing it took months, however, from the early fall of 1776 until the spring of 1777.

Several factors caused the delay. Because the war was still on, members of the legislature were often absent for military duty. Also, some lawmakers deliberately stalled the proceedings, feeling that creating something as important as the political structure of the state should wait for more tranquil times.

The constitution that New York's lawmakers finally approved used many ideas that are now fundamentals of American-style democracy. Among them are self-government by the people through elected officials, limits on government powers, a balance between the governor's office and other legislative branches, and a guarantee of religious freedom.

Voting

Self-government was perhaps the most crucial point lawmakers considered. Fair representation, after all, was a primary reason the war was being fought.

A ballot system, designed to go into effect after the war's end, was approved. The main requirement for voting concerned property. Any man who owned land valued at twenty pounds beyond his debts, or who rented land with an annual value of at least forty shillings, was eligible. (Women could not vote, and the nation did not adopt the dollar as official currency until 1785.)

This law effectively shifted the balance of power from the cities to the countryside. As more new settlers arrived in the countryside, the number of New Yorkers who met the landowning qualifications increased. At the same time, the number of voters shrank within the ranks of small shopkeepers, artisans, and workmen in New York City and other cities.

General George Clinton became New York's first governor in 1777.

The New York Constitution was formally adopted on April 20, 1777. The colony officially became the state of New York, and Kingston was named as the first state capital. (The capital was moved to Albany in 1797.)

Elections and appointments were held in the spring and summer of 1777, and the legislature convened for the first time in September. George Clinton, a

Colonists gather in the streets of New York City as George Washington is inaugurated as the first president of the United States.

general on active duty, became the state's first governor and eventually served five terms in that office.

The reaction to the constitution among New Yorkers was mixed. Some found it too democratic, others too conservative, but many considered it model legislation. Alexander Hamilton, a New Yorker prominent in federal politics, wrote to a New York lawmaker, Gouverneur Morris, that "on the whole ... I think your Government far the best that we have yet seen, and capable of giving long and substantial happiness to the people." [25]

New York City: The Nation's Capital

In the wake of the end of the war, American lawmakers set about creating a national government. America was originally organized as a loose confederation, rather than a federation with a strong central government. In 1787 the Congress of the Confederation drafted a landmark in American legislation: the U.S. Constitution. New York was the eleventh state to endorse it, in June 1788.

The Congress convened in several cities before moving to New York City and designating it as the first capital of the United States. In April 1789 George Washington was inaugurated there as the nation's first president.

The city, badly damaged during the war, had spent a fortune upgrading so that it would be worthy of serving as the nation's capital.

Remodeling City Hall into Federal Hall alone cost nearly $100,000, an enormous sum in those days.

New Yorkers' objections were strong, therefore, when lawmakers decided in 1790 to create a new location, the District of Columbia, to serve as the nation's capital.

Despite the time and money that had gone into renovations, New York City was in many ways still in very poor shape. It had inadequate water supplies, little or no paving, and no sewer system. Garbage was fed to pigs that wandered the streets, as they had been doing since Dutch days; human waste was carried in buckets to the city's rivers by servants and slaves.

Given this poor condition and the loss of its status as the nation's capital, some people predicted that the city would collapse, or at best suffer greatly, once the seat of government moved. But the superiority of New York City's harbor helped it maintain its importance as a seaport and overall the city remained strong. Historian Bruce Bliven Jr. notes, "The city adjusted to its losses."[26]

More Land and People

Population, in the city and in New York overall, rose dramatically in the postwar years. By 1790, the year of the first federal census, New York City had become the biggest urban center in the country, with 33,000 people. Meanwhile, according to that same census, over 300,000 residents now lived in the state. Most had come to take advantage of the vast new tracts of land opening up in New York's northern, central, and western regions.

This land became available because the government had begun selling off publicly held land at bargain prices. During the late 1780s New York's land commissioners sold more than 5.5 million acres in the northern and central parts of the state.

Some of the land handed out was awarded to war veterans, who had each been promised 600-acre parcels for their part in the conflict. More than 1.5 million acres were set aside for veterans. The veterans were not required to settle on their land, however, and many sold their shares.

Much of this newly available acreage came from the property of Loyalists. These landowners fled the colony after the war to avoid repressive laws, such as heavy taxes, as well as open hostility from their

Trade ships crowd New York City's harbor after the Revolutionary War. Population growth after the war allowed New York to become the biggest urban center in the newly formed country.

Patriot neighbors. Loyalists were frequently tarred and feathered, flogged, or run out of town at the hands of angry Patriots.

Some Loyalists had been wealthy, aristocratic owners of large tracts of land. Many, however, had simply been farmers and small landowners. In either case, their land was confiscated by the state government and resold or awarded to veterans.

New Settlers

The prospect of settling the fertile farmland of upstate and western New York attracted settlers from many countries in Europe, especially Ireland, France, and Germany. Still more came from a closer locale— just across the border in New England.

Former New Englanders had already settled much of eastern Long Island, and for more than a decade they had steadily populated several of New York's counties. After 1783, however, they began arriving in large numbers.

They came on foot or by ship, sled, and oxcart in a genuine land rush. In a single three-day period in February 1795, twelve hundred sleighs carrying New Englanders and their possessions passed through Albany on the way to farms in Genesee County in the western part of the state.

The Burr-Hamilton Duel

One tragic aspect of New York politics was the rivalry between two prominent politicians, Alexander Hamilton and Aaron Burr. The rivalry ended in a duel that left Hamilton dead and Burr disgraced.

Hamilton was a delegate to the Constitutional Convention and first secretary of the treasury. Burr was a U.S. senator and the third vice president. Both were brilliant, ambitious men who bitterly hated each other. Besides a personal dislike, the men had opposing views on the future of the country: Hamilton favored a strong central government, while Burr preferred giving more power to individual states.

The end of their long-running battle came in 1804, when Hamilton allegedly made remarks at a dinner party in which he outlined his "despicable opinion" of Burr and called Burr dangerous. A furious Burr challenged Hamilton to a duel. Hamilton was reluctant—he had lost a son in a duel only a few years before—but felt honor-bound to accept.

The duel was held at Weehawken, New Jersey, because dueling was forbidden in New York. Hamilton was killed. He left his wife and seven children heavily in debt, which friends helped to pay off.

Arrest warrants on a charge of treason were issued. Burr fled and was arrested in 1807. His trial ended in acquittal, but Burr remained under a cloud of suspicion and fled to Europe, where he tried to interest Napoleon in mounting an invasion of Florida. Four years later he returned to New York to practice law. He died in 1836.

Alexander Hamilton is shot by rival Aaron Burr in their famous duel.

The Iroquois and other Indian nations in New York fared badly during this period of expansion. According to an agreement made in 1768, the Iroquois still technically owned vast stretches of land. However, the Indians had been severely weakened during the war. Most, including the Iroquois, had sided with the British.

A few thousand Indians weakened by war were no match for the pressures put upon them by hundreds of thousands of eager settlers. The Iroquois were steadily forced to give up more and more of their remaining land. Other tribes, including the Seneca, Cayuga, and Onondaga, also made vast concessions.

By 1800 almost no land in the entire state was under Indian rule. The once-strong union that banded the Iroquois nations together had essentially dissolved under the dual pressures of war and encroaching Europeans. Historian Michael Kammen notes, "The effect of the war upon the Six Nations was to shatter [their] old unity.... The impact of the peace would deprive the Iroquois of almost all their territorial inheritance. If the American Revolution helped to create a great nation, it also served to complete the destruction of another."[27]

Boom Economy

The increase in immigration brought boom times for the state's economy. Fortunes were lost and won in an intense market in land speculation. Land scouts did a brisk business in finding suitable land for settlers, for which they received a commission. The state's import and export trade, and businesses related to it, were especially robust in the years after the war, in large part because of a conflict that took place far away. The Napoleonic Wars began in 1792, pitting France against a shifting coalition of other European countries.

The effect of these wars on the fledgling United States was dramatic. In 1792, the total value of exports from New York was about $2.5 million. By 1807 that figure had increased by more than ten times, to $26 million. The jump can be attributed to France's—as well as its enemies'—desperate need for goods, because trade with other European countries was severely limited. Both sides turned to New York City's import-export industry for help.

As import-export mushroomed, the city acquired the basics of a solid financial center. In 1792 its first bank, the Bank of New York, was established, and that same year an out-of-doors meeting of twenty-four stockbrokers on Wall Street organized what is now the New York Stock Exchange. New York City was quickly able to cement its position as the state's—and the nation's—primary financial center.

Into the Future

The boom times and expansion continued into the new century for New York. By 1800 it had become the second-largest and most populous state in the Union, trailing only Virginia. Ten years later, it was the largest—not only in population, diversity, size, and growth, but also in manufacturing, trade, and transportation.

Transportation was the key to any economy that relied on shipping its goods. One reason New York continued to prosper was that it was blessed with an extensive network of waterways—rivers, lakes, and sea channels—that made transporting goods relatively easy.

A major step forward in transportation was made in New York when an inventor, Robert Fulton, tested his revolutionary design for a steamboat in 1807. The ship's first major test run was made between New York City and Albany. Sailing sloops required four days to make the 150-mile run from New York to Albany; Fulton's steamboat did it in only thirty-two hours. In the years to come, Fulton's invention

Inventor Robert Fulton's steamboat makes its way down a river. The ship's speed and efficiency changed the import-export and transportation industries forever.

Crowds gather at the 1825 opening of the Erie Canal. The canal opened up many trade and transportation opportunities for New York.

radically improved the speed and efficiency with which goods could be shipped from one part of the country to another.

Improvements in roads and turnpikes also dramatically changed New York's economy and patterns of settlement in the years after the war. As more and better roads spread westward from locations along the Hudson River, settlers were able to move across the state with greater ease. What had once been long, exhausting journeys became relatively simple.

Interrupted temporarily by the War of 1812, New York's expansion continued. The opening of the Erie Canal in 1825, connecting the Great Lakes with New York City via the Hudson River, confirmed

New York's position as the main gateway to the newly opened lands of the Midwest.

New York had always been one of the more important of the original thirteen colonies. Now, as the United States moved from being a brand-new country to being a powerful nation, New York's role became that of one of the most important states in the Union.

Notes

Introduction: New York Colony

1. Quoted in Jon Butler, *Becoming America: The Revolution Before 1776*. Cambridge, MA: Harvard University Press, 2000, p. 185.
2. Quoted in Michael Kammen, *Colonial New York*. White Plains, NY: KTO Press, 1987, p. 369.

Chapter One: The Origins of New York Colony

3. Quoted in Bruce Bliven Jr., *New York: A History*. New York: W. W. Norton, 1981, p. 12.
4. Quoted in Kammen, *Colonial New York*, p. 1.
5. Quoted in Francis Parkman, *The Francis Parkman Reader*. New York: Da Capo Press, 1998, p. 149.
6. Arthur Quinn, *A New World: An Epic of Colonial America from the Founding of Jamestown to the Fall of Quebec*. Boston: Faber & Faber, 1994, p. 188.
7. Allan Keller, *Colonial America: A Compact History*. New York: Hawthorn Books, 1971, p. 38.
8. Quoted in Quinn, *A New World*, p. 195.

Chapter Two: Forming the Colony

9. Quoted in Kammen, *Colonial New York*, p. 71.
10. Kammen, *Colonial New York*, p. 151.
11. Kammen, *Colonial New York*, p. 330.

Chapter Three: Daily Life in the Colony

12. Quoted in Arthur M. Schlesinger, *The Birth of the Nation*. Boston: Houghton Mifflin, 1968, p. 156.
13. Bliven Jr., *New York: A History*, p. 31.
14. Schlesinger, *The Birth of the Nation*, p. 39.
15. Schlesinger, *The Birth of the Nation*, pp. 22–23.
16. Quoted in Kammen, *Colonial New York*, p. 155.
17. Quoted in Schlesinger, *The Birth of the Nation*, p. 136.
18. Quoted in Schlesinger, *The Birth of the Nation*, p. 24.

Chapter Four: New York's Role in the Revolution

19. Quoted in Bliven Jr., *New York: A History*, pp. 38–39.
20. Quoted in Ray Raphael, *A People's History of the American Revolution*. New York: New Press, 2001, p. 3.
21. Bliven Jr., *New York: A History*, p. 54.
22. Quoted in Kammen, *Colonial New York*, p. 342.
23. Bliven Jr., *New York: A History*, p. 79.
24. Quoted in Bliven Jr., *New York: A History*, p. 82.

Chapter Five: New York After the Revolution

25. Quoted in Kammen, *Colonial New York*, p. 375.
26. Bliven Jr., *New York: A History*, p. 91.
27. Kammen, *Colonial New York*, p. 373.

Chronology

1609
Henry Hudson explores the Hudson River for Holland.

1613
First Dutch traders arrive in New Netherland.

1623
New Netherland formally declared a province of Holland.

1626
Director-general Peter Minuit purchases the island of Manhattan.

1644
Peter Stuyvesant becomes director-general of New Netherland.

1664
England claims New Netherland for itself; Roger Nicolls becomes the colony's governor and renames it New York.

1689
Jacob Leisler leads the rebellion named after him.

1765
Protests held against the Stamp Act.

1774
New York Patriots stage their own Tea Party and organize the first New York Assembly.

1775
George Washington is appointed commander in chief of the American armed forces.

1776
Washington orders the barricading of New York City, but after a bloody battle the British occupy it; Declaration of Independence issued.

1777
The Battle of Saratoga, a victory for the Patriots, is a turning point in the war; the New York Assembly adopts a state constitution; the first state governor and other lawmakers are elected and appointed.

1781
British forces in America surrender.

1783
The Revolutionary War formally ends with the signing of the Treaty of Paris.

1788
New York endorses the U.S. Constitution.

1789
New York City becomes the nation's first capital; George Washington is inaugurated as the first president of the United States.

1790
Congress chooses Washington, D.C., as the nation's permanent capital; the first federal census finds that New York City is the largest city in the United States.

1800
The federal census finds that New York is the second largest state in the union.

For Further Reading

Alan Axelrod, *The Complete Idiot's Guide to the American Revolution*. Indianapolis, IN: Alpha Books, 2000. Despite the overly cutesy tone, this is a good introduction to the subject, with lots of interesting trivia.

Laurie M. Carlson, *Colonial Kids: An Activity Guide to Life in the New World*. Chicago: Chicago Review Press, 1997. A book of activities that re-create aspects of daily life in the colonies.

Kieran Doherty, *Puritans, Pilgrims, and Merchants: Founders of the Northeast Colonies*. Minneapolis, MN: Oliver Press, 1999. This entertaining and informative book contains one chapter on Peter Stuyvesant of the Dutch colony of New Netherlands.

Howard Egger-Bovet and Marlene Smith-Baranzini, *Brown Paper School US Kids History: Book of the American Colonies*. Boston: Little, Brown, 1996. A book of text, drawings, and activities designed to bring the colonies alive.

Joy Hakim, *From Colonies to Country*. New York: Oxford University Press, 1993. This lively book is part of the *A History of US* series.

Albert Marrin, *George Washington and the Founding of a Nation*. New York: Dutton, 2001. A well-written biography for young adults, tracing Washington's role in the years before, during, and after the Revolutionary War.

Carolyn Kott Washburn, *A Multicultural Portrait of Colonial Life*. New York: Marshall Cavendish, 1994. A book with a strong emphasis on the daily lives of Native Americans and African slaves during the Colonial period.

Works Consulted

Bruce Bliven Jr., *New York: A History*. New York: W. W. Norton, 1981. This volume in a series on the United States in honor of the Bicentennial is a charming, anecdotal history.

Jon Butler, *Becoming America: The Revolution Before 1776*. Cambridge, MA: Harvard University Press, 2000. An excellent general history of the economy and peoples of the colonies.

John E. Findling and Frank W. Thackeray, ed., *Events That Changed America in the Eighteenth Century*. Westport, CT: Greenwood Press, 1998. A textbook on specific aspects of political events.

Michael Kammen, *Colonial New York*. White Plains, NY: KTO Press, 1987. A massive and scholarly history.

Allan Keller, *Colonial America: A Compact History*. New York: Hawthorn Books, 1971. A good one-volume popular history.

Ted Morgan, *Wilderness at Dawn: The Settling of the North American Continent*. New York: Simon & Schuster, 1993. An extensively researched and well-written account by a distinguished historian.

Francis Parkman, *The Francis Parkman Reader*. New York: Da Capo Press, 1998. A collection of writings by a famed historian who is best known as a scholar of the conflict between the French and the British in the New World.

Arthur Quinn, *A New World: An Epic of Colonial America from the Founding of Jamestown to the Fall of Quebec*. Boston: Faber & Faber, 1994. An anecdotal history written by a professor at the University of California at Berkeley.

Ray Raphael, *A People's History of the American Revolution*. New York: New Press, 2001. A fascinating book that uses the words of ordinary people of the time to reconstruct the Revolutionary War era.

Arthur M. Schlesinger, *The Birth of the Nation*. Boston: Houghton Mifflin, 1968. An excellent book by one of America's most distinguished historians.

Index

Picture Credits

Cover photo: Carwitham/Mary Evans Picture Library

© Bettmann/CORBIS, 15, 22, 26, 33, 50, 66, 67

© CORBIS, 11, 49, 56

Cornell University Library/Library of Congress, 16, 60

Dover Publications, 30, 51, 61

© Catherine Karnow/CORBIS, 39

Library of Congress, 17, 19, 42, 52, 55, 64

North Wind Picture Archives, 24, 29, 32, 36, 40, 63

© Elizabeth Whiting & Associates/CORBIS, 43

About the Author

Adam Woog is the author of nearly thirty books for adults and young adults. He lives with his wife and daughter in his hometown of Seattle, Washington.